HAL LEONARD STUDENT PIANO LIBRARY

BOOK 3 • INTERMEDIATE

Piano Recital Showcase

10 FAVORITE PIECES CAREFULLY SELECTED FOR INTERMEDIATE LEVEL

CONTENTS

ISBN 978-1-4234-5659-9

HAL•LEONARD®
CORPORATION
7777 W. BLUEMOUND RD. P.O. BOX 13819 MILWAUKEE, WI 53213

In Australia Contact:
Hal Leonard Australia Pty. Ltd.
4 Lentara Court
Cheltenham, Victoria, 3192 Australia
Email: ausadmin@halleonard.com.au

Visit Hal Leonard Online at
www.halleonard.com

Castilian Dreamer

By Carol Klose

Andante (♩ = 80)

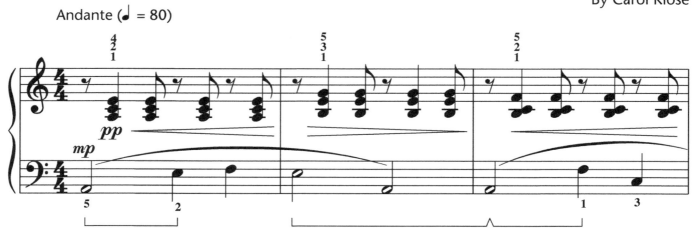

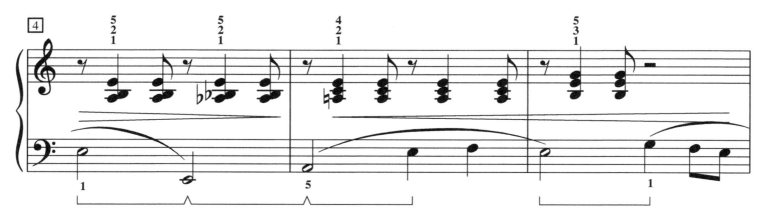

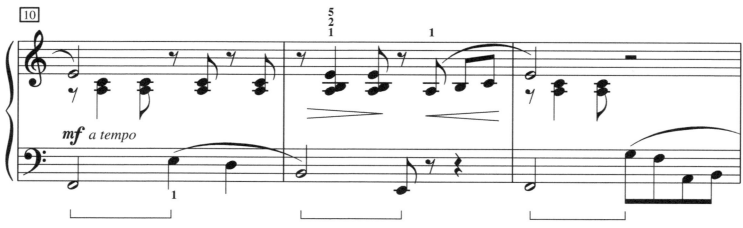

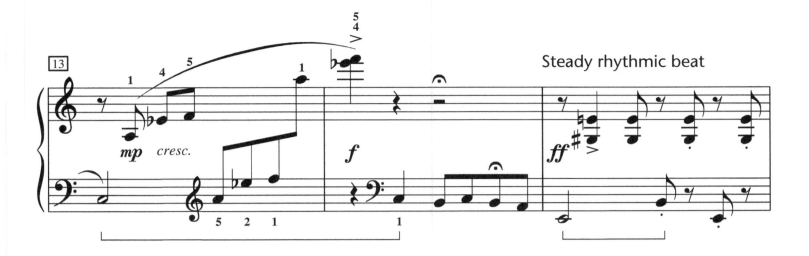

Steady rhythmic beat

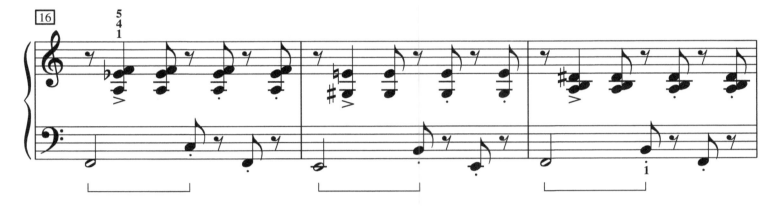

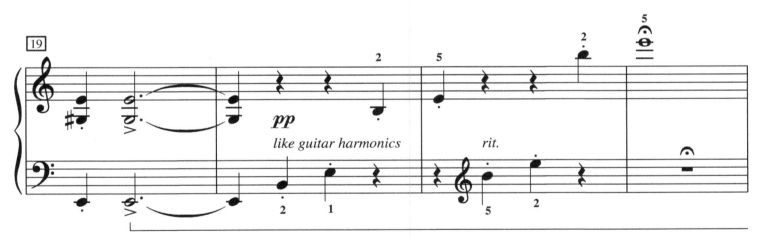

like guitar harmonics

rit.

Slightly slower than beginning tempo (♩ = 72)

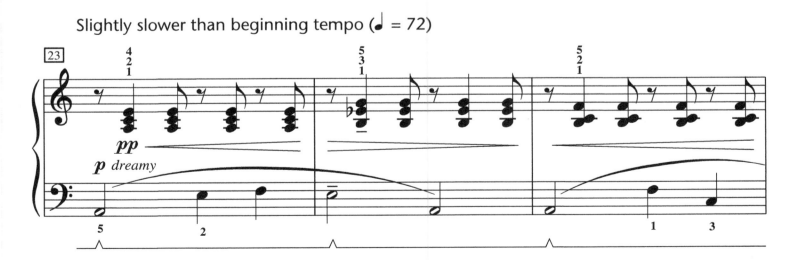

pp

p dreamy

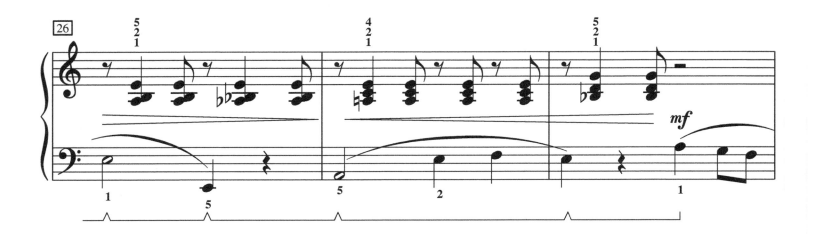

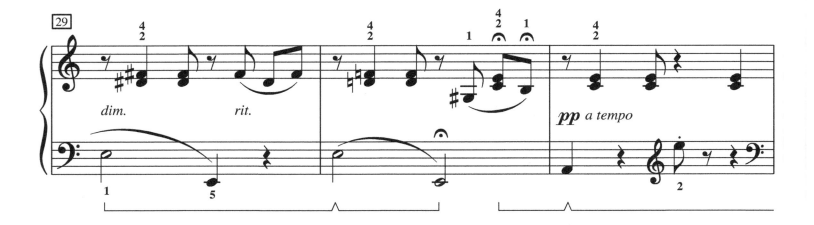

Slower, with determination

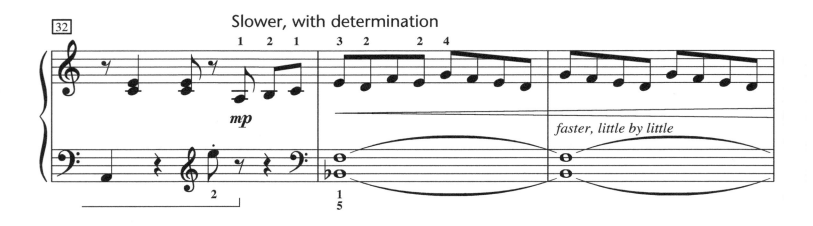

faster, little by little

Slowly

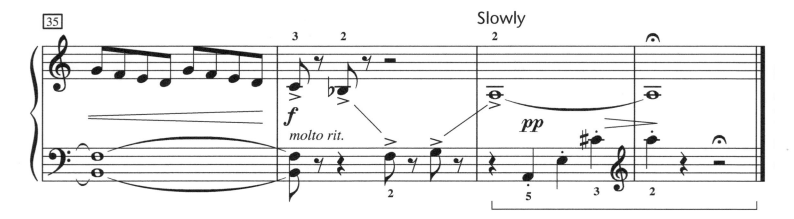

Jump Around Rag

By Bill Boyd

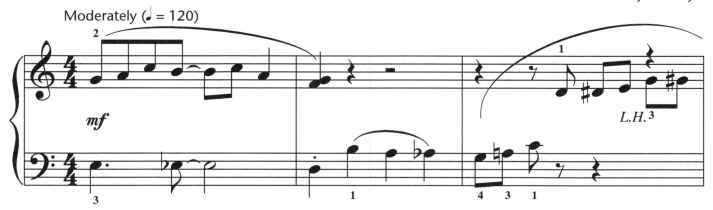

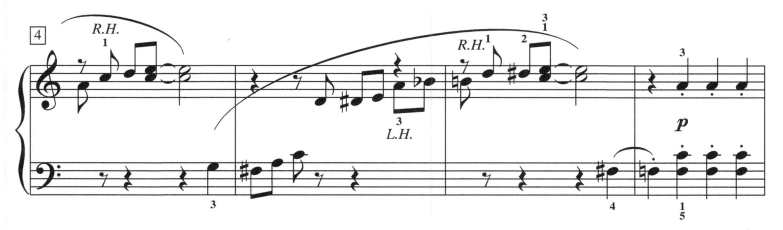

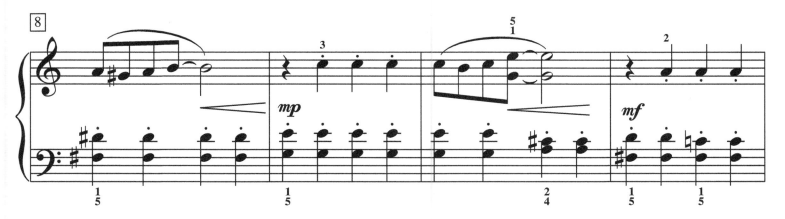

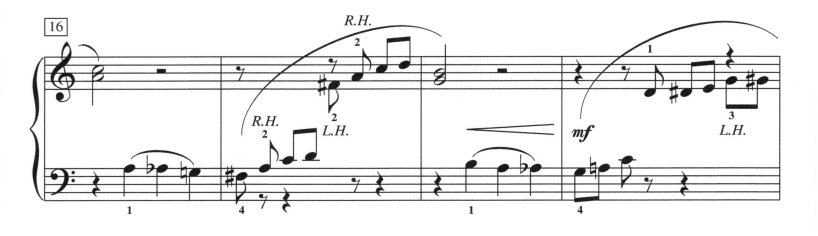

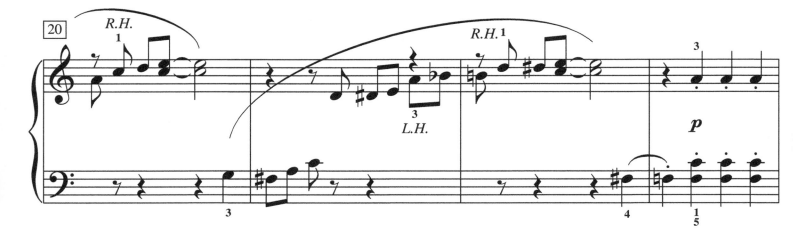

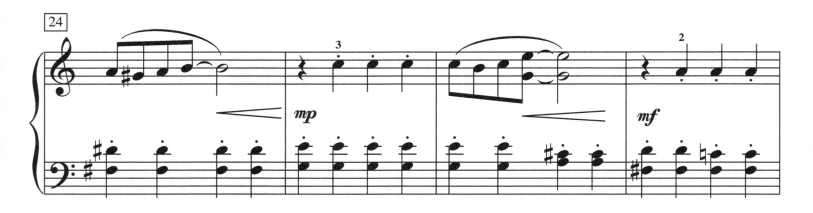

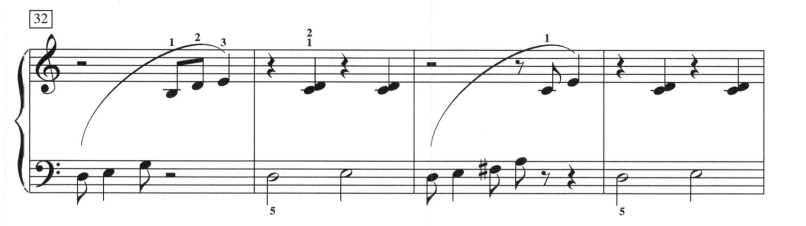

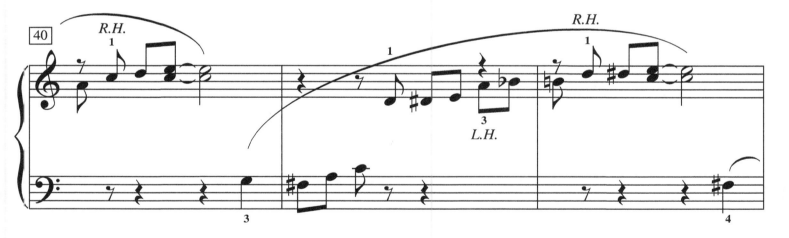

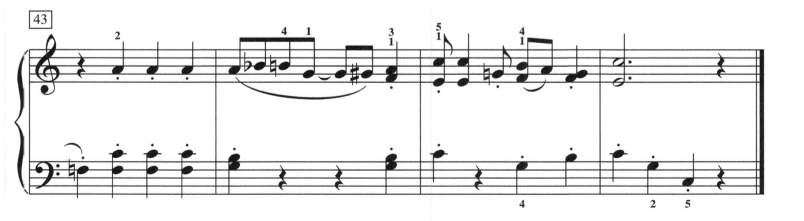

Dreaming Song

By Tony Caramia

Slowly and pensively (♩ = 100-120)

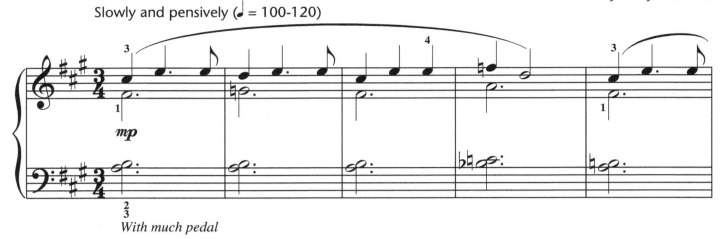

With much pedal

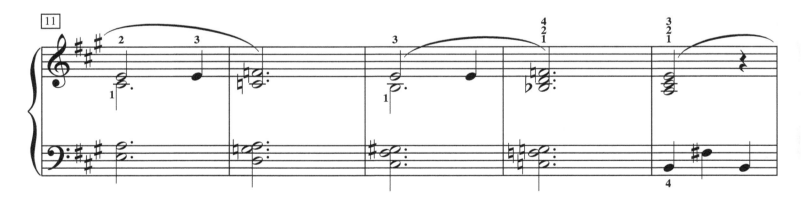

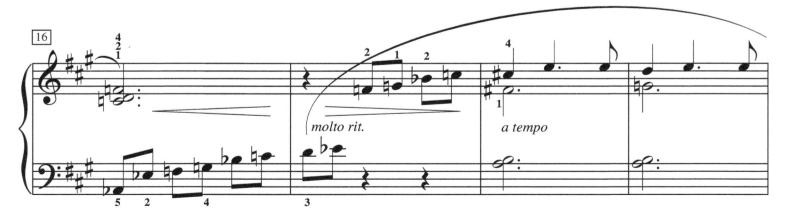

diminuendo

*slower and softer
to the end*

Little Mazurka

By Christos Tsitsaros

2nd time D.C. al Fine

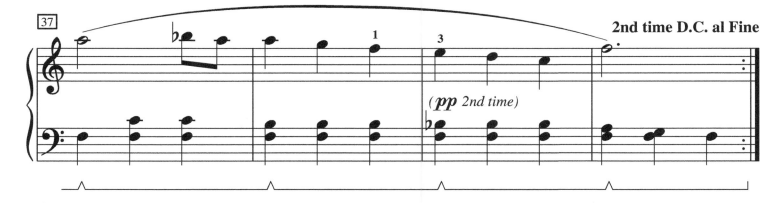

Meaghan's Melody

By Jennifer Linn

With a bit of lilt (♩. = 56)

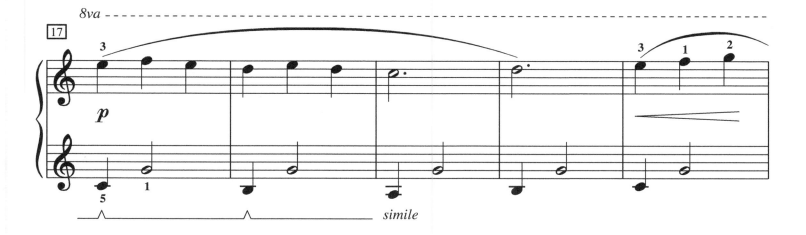

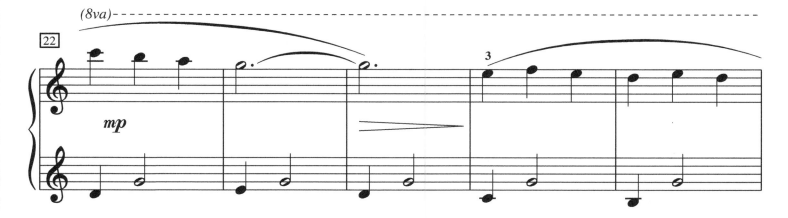

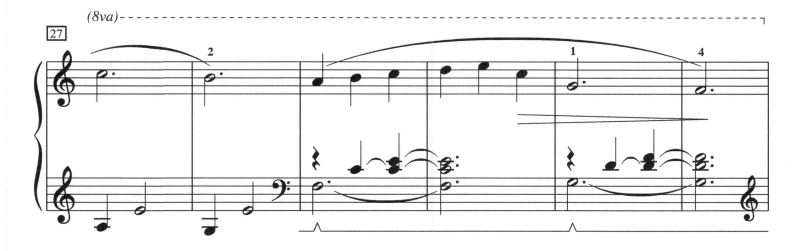

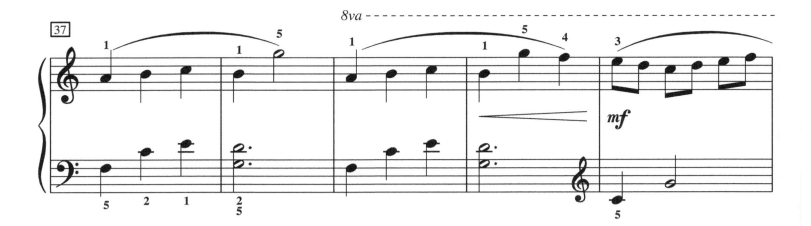

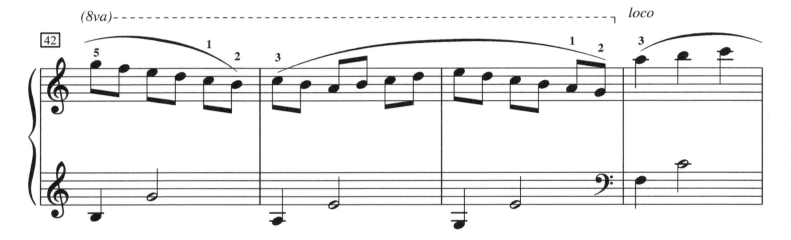

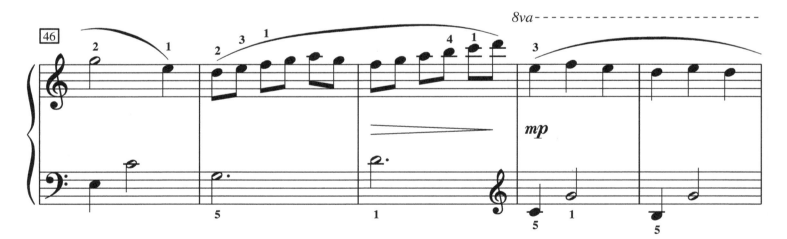

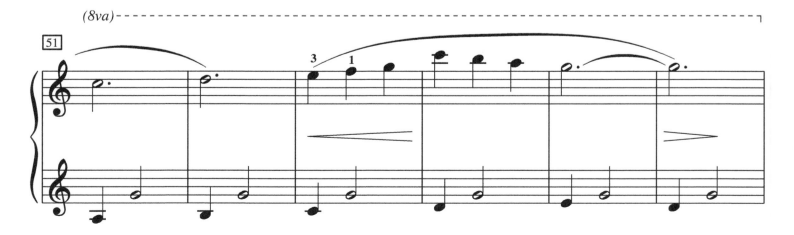

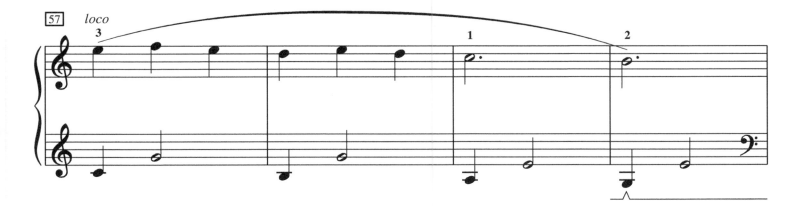

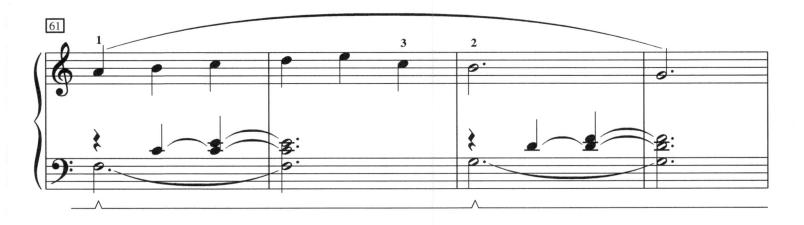

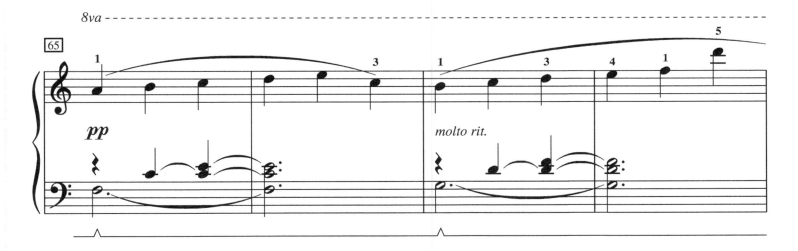

Mountain Splendor

By Mona Rejino

Freely, with expression (♩ = ca.132)

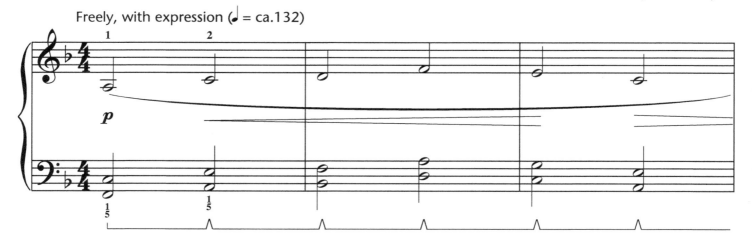

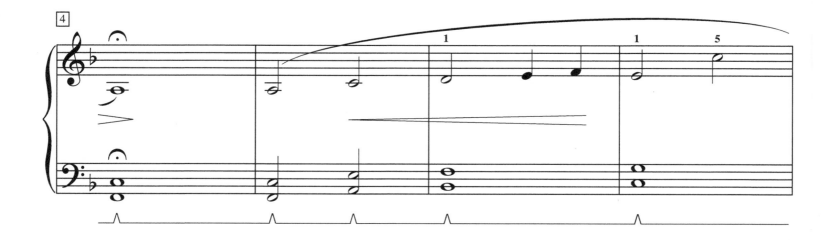

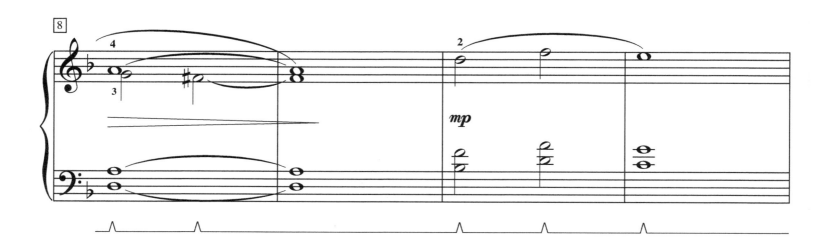

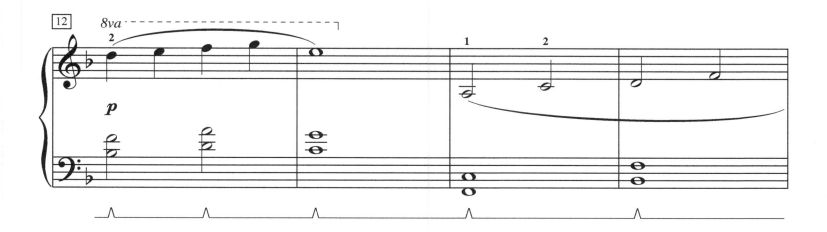

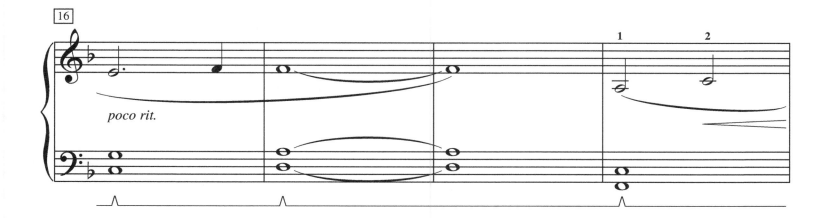

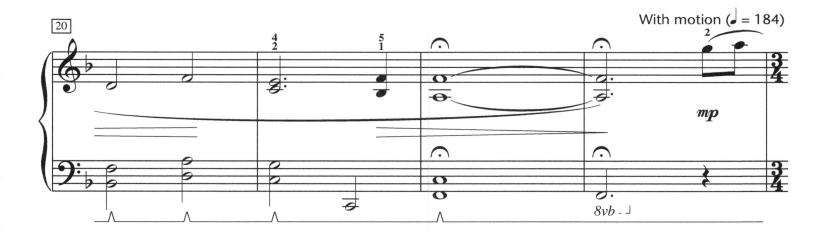

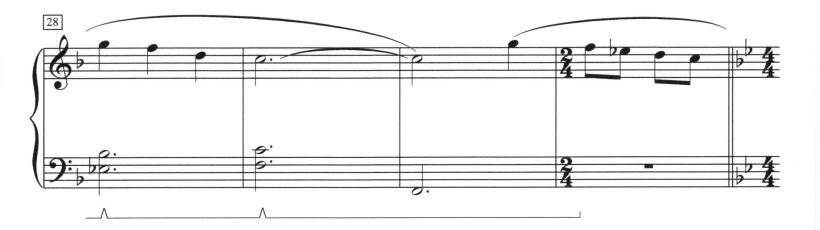

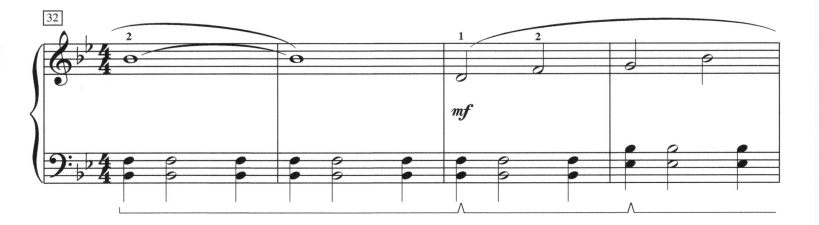

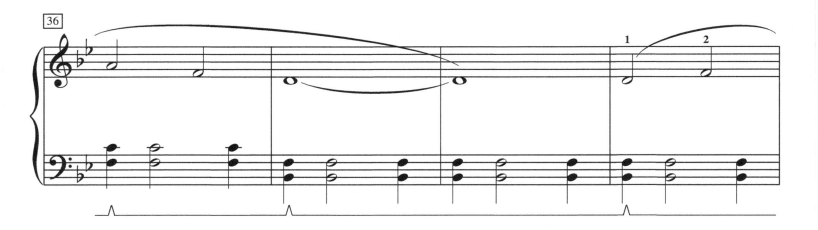

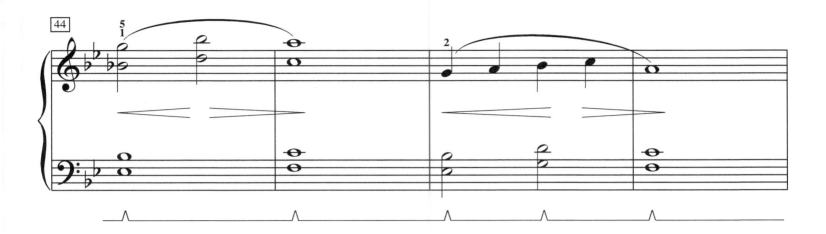

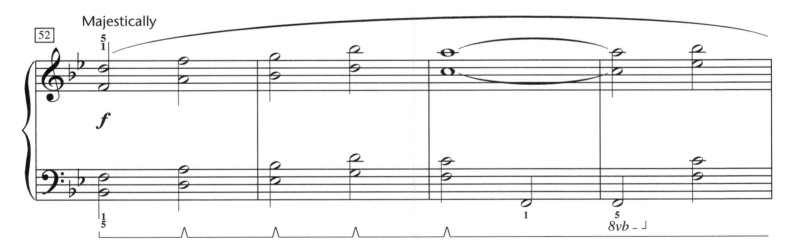

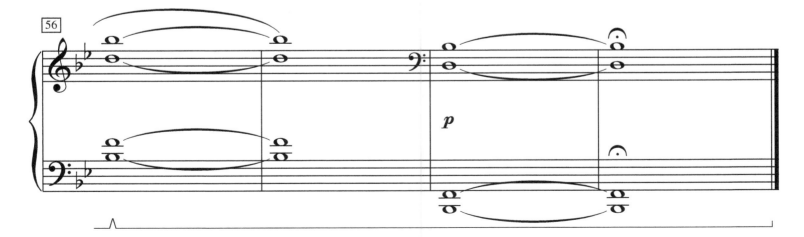

Seaside Stride

By Mike Springer

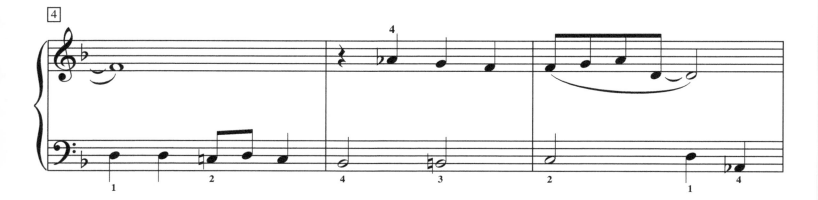

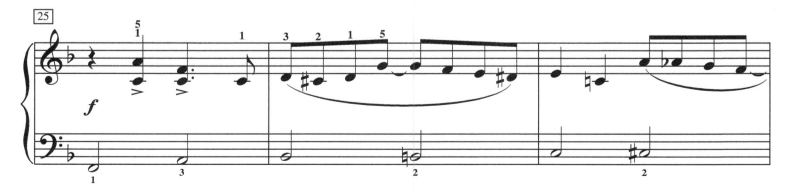

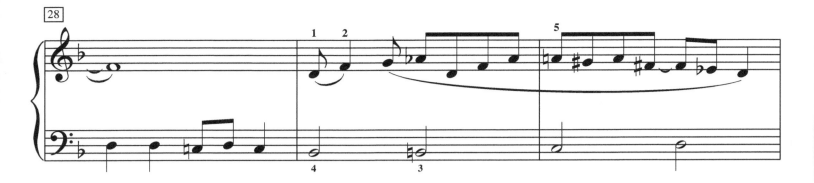

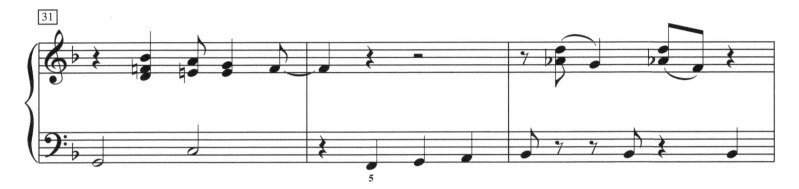

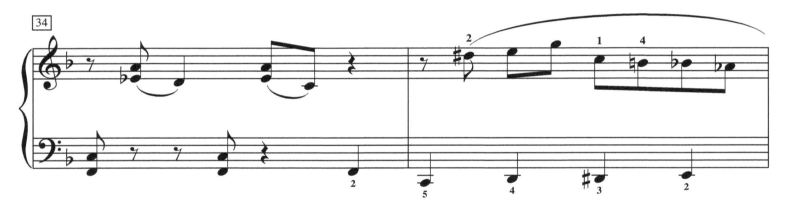

22

Snap to It!

By Mona Rejino

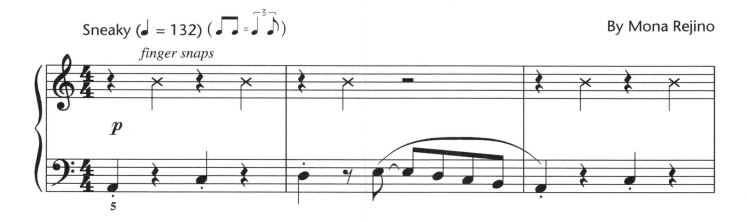

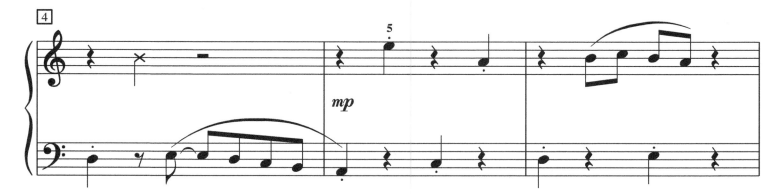

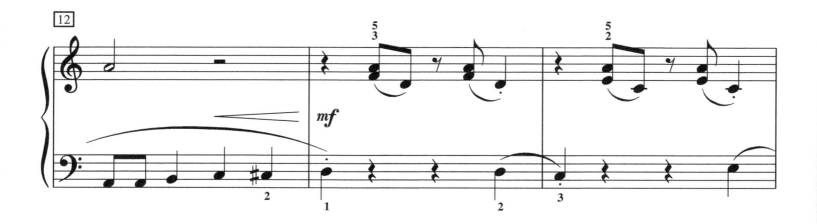

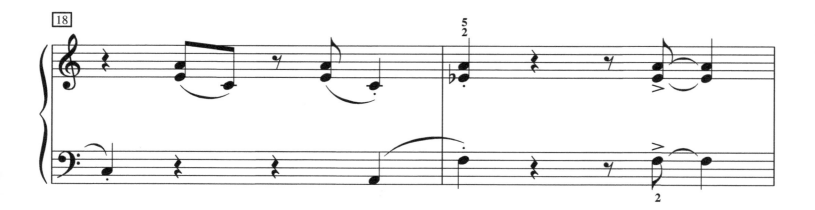

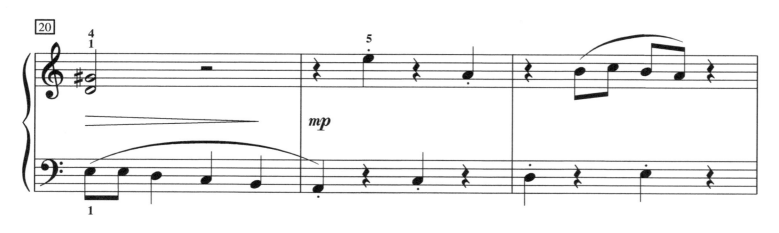

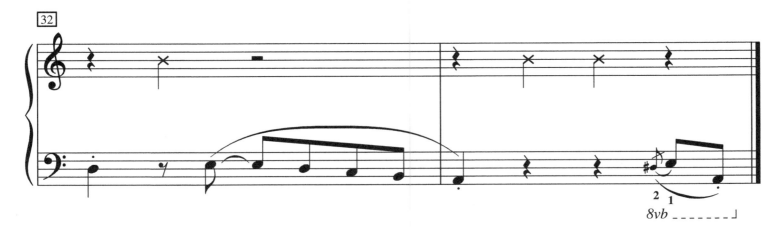

Too Cool to Fool

By Bill Boyd

Moderate Rock (♩ = 138)

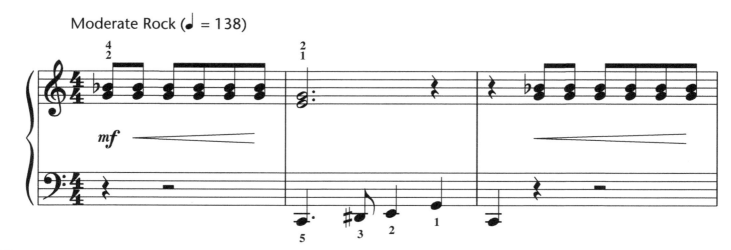

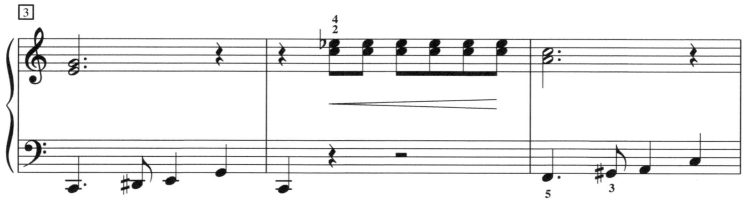

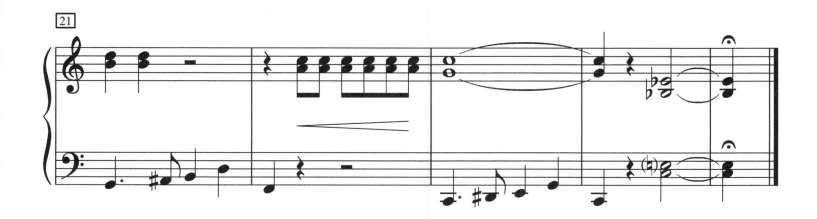

Wizard's Wish

By Jennifer Linn

With great imagination (♩ = 126)

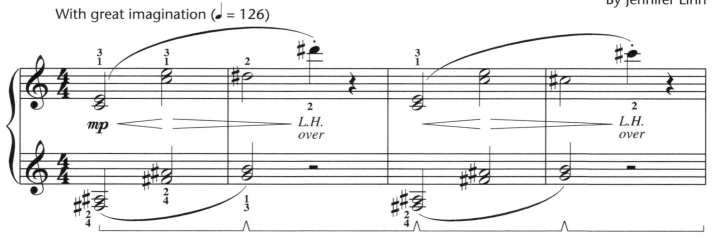

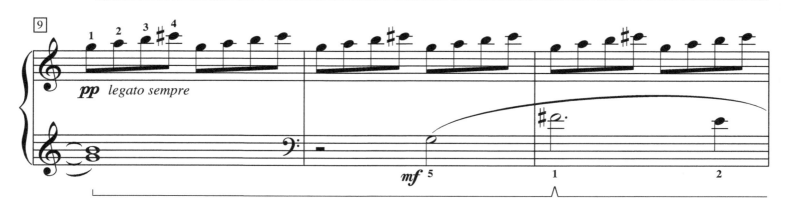

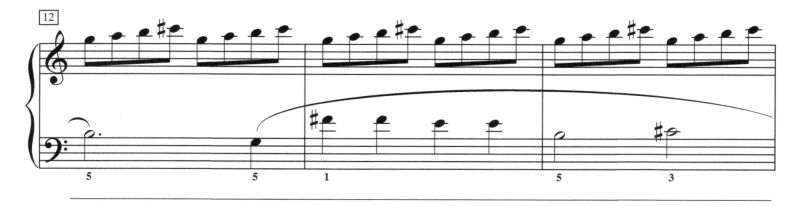

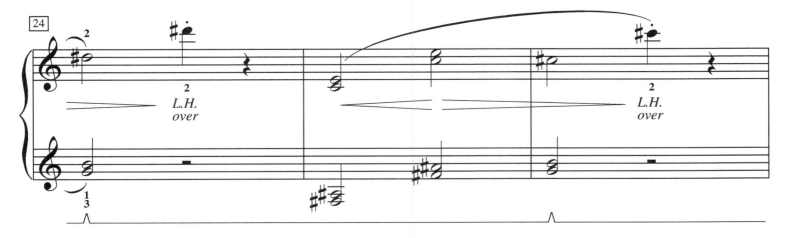

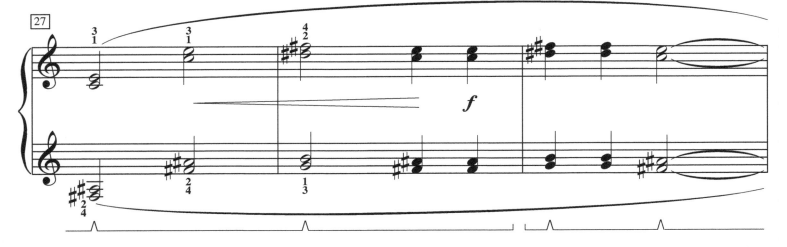

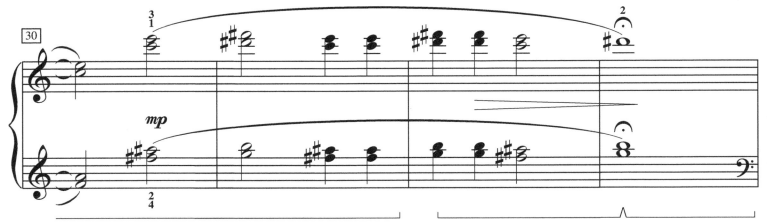

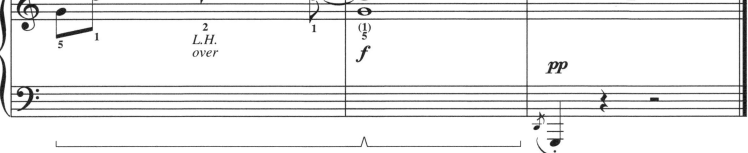

This series showcases great original piano music from our **Hal Leonard Student Piano Library** family of composers. Carefully graded for easy selection.

BILL BOYD

JAZZ BITS (AND PIECES)
Early Intermediate Level
00290312 11 Solos......................$7.99

JAZZ DELIGHTS
Intermediate Level
00240435 11 Solos......................$8.99

JAZZ FEST
Intermediate Level
00240436 10 Solos......................$8.99

JAZZ PRELIMS
Early Elementary Level
00290032 12 Solos......................$7.99

JAZZ SKETCHES
Intermediate Level
00220001 8 Solos........................$8.99

JAZZ STARTERS
Elementary Level
00290425 10 Solos......................$8.99

JAZZ STARTERS II
Late Elementary Level
00290434 11 Solos......................$7.99

JAZZ STARTERS III
Late Elementary Level
00290465 12 Solos......................$8.99

THINK JAZZ!
Early Intermediate Level
00290417 Method Book............$12.99

TONY CARAMIA

JAZZ MOODS
Intermediate Level
00296728 8 Solos........................$6.95

SUITE DREAMS
Intermediate Level
00296775 4 Solos........................$6.99

SONDRA CLARK

DAKOTA DAYS
Intermediate Level
00296521 5 Solos........................$6.95

FLORIDA FANTASY SUITE
Intermediate Level
00296766 3 Duets.......................$7.95

THREE ODD METERS
Intermediate Level
00296472 3 Duets.......................$6.95

MATTHEW EDWARDS

**CONCERTO FOR
YOUNG PIANISTS**
FOR 2 PIANOS, FOUR HANDS
Intermediate Level Book/CD
00296356 3 Movements $19.99

CONCERTO NO. 2 IN G MAJOR
FOR 2 PIANOS, 4 HANDS
Intermediate Level Book/CD
00296670 3 Movements............$17.99

PHILLIP KEVEREN

MOUSE ON A MIRROR
Late Elementary Level
00296361 5 Solos........................$8.99

MUSICAL MOODS
Elementary/Late Elementary Level
00296714 7 Solos........................$6.99

SHIFTY-EYED BLUES
Late Elementary Level
00296374 5 Solos........................$7.99

CAROL KLOSE

THE BEST OF CAROL KLOSE
Early to Late Intermediate Level
00146151 15 Solos....................$12.99

CORAL REEF SUITE
Late Elementary Level
00296354 7 Solos........................$7.50

DESERT SUITE
Intermediate Level
00296667 6 Solos........................$7.99

FANCIFUL WALTZES
Early Intermediate Level
00296473 5 Solos........................$7.95

GARDEN TREASURES
Late Intermediate Level
00296787 5 Solos........................$8.50

ROMANTIC EXPRESSIONS
Intermediate to Late Intermediate Level
00296923 5 Solos........................$8.99

WATERCOLOR MINIATURES
Early Intermediate Level
00296848 7 Solos........................$7.99

JENNIFER LINN

AMERICAN IMPRESSIONS
Intermediate Level
00296471 6 Solos........................$8.99

ANIMALS HAVE FEELINGS TOO
Early Elementary/Elementary Level
00147789 8 Solos........................$8.99

AU CHOCOLAT
Late Elementary/Early Intermediate Level
00298110 7 Solos........................$8.99

CHRISTMAS IMPRESSIONS
Intermediate Level
00296706 8 Solos........................$8.99

JUST PINK
Elementary Level
00296722 9 Solos........................$8.99

LES PETITES IMAGES
Late Elementary Level
00296664 7 Solos........................$8.99

LES PETITES IMPRESSIONS
Intermediate Level
00296355 6 Solos........................$8.99

REFLECTIONS
Late Intermediate Level
00296843 5 Solos........................$8.99

TALES OF MYSTERY
Intermediate Level
00296769 6 Solos........................$8.99

LYNDA LYBECK-ROBINSON

ALASKA SKETCHES
Early Intermediate Level
00119637 8 Solos........................$8.99

AN AWESOME ADVENTURE
Late Elementary Level
00137563 8 Solos........................$7.99

FOR THE BIRDS
Early Intermediate/Intermediate Level
00237078 9 Solos........................$8.99

WHISPERING WOODS
Late Elementary Level
00275905 9 Solos........................$8.99

MONA REJINO

CIRCUS SUITE
Late Elementary Level
00296665 5 Solos........................$8.99

COLOR WHEEL
Early Intermediate Level
00201951 6 Solos........................$9.99

IMPRESIONES DE ESPAÑA
Intermediate Level
00337520 6 Solos........................$8.99

IMPRESSIONS OF NEW YORK
Intermediate Level
00364212................................$8.99

JUST FOR KIDS
Elementary Level
00296840 8 Solos........................$7.99

MERRY CHRISTMAS MEDLEYS
Intermediate Level
00296799 5 Solos........................$8.99

MINIATURES IN STYLE
Intermediate Level
00148088 6 Solos........................$8.99

PORTRAITS IN STYLE
Early Intermediate Level
00296507 6 Solos........................$8.99

EUGÉNIE ROCHEROLLE

CELEBRATION SUITE
Intermediate Level
00152724 3 Duets.......................$8.99

**ENCANTOS ESPAÑOLES
(SPANISH DELIGHTS)**
Intermediate Level
00125451 6 Solos........................$8.99

JAMBALAYA
Intermediate Level
00296654 2 Pianos, 8 Hands.....$12.99
00296725 2 Pianos, 4 Hands.......$7.95

JEROME KERN CLASSICS
Intermediate Level
00296577 10 Solos....................$12.99

LITTLE BLUES CONCERTO
Early Intermediate Level
00142801 2 Pianos, 4 Hands......$12.99

TOUR FOR TWO
Late Elementary Level
00296832 6 Duets.......................$9.99

TREASURES
Late Elementary/Early Intermediate Level
00296924 7 Solos........................$8.99

JEREMY SISKIND

BIG APPLE JAZZ
Intermediate Level
00278209 8 Solos........................$8.99

MYTHS AND MONSTERS
Late Elementary/Early Intermediate Level
00148148 9 Solos........................$8.99

CHRISTOS TSITSAROS

**DANCES FROM AROUND
THE WORLD**
Early Intermediate Level
00296688 7 Solos........................$8.99

FIVE SUMMER PIECES
Late Intermediate/Advanced Level
00361235 5 Solos......................$12.99

LYRIC BALLADS
Intermediate/Late Intermediate Level
00102404 6 Solos........................$8.99

POETIC MOMENTS
Intermediate Level
00296403 8 Solos........................$8.99

SEA DIARY
Early Intermediate Level
00253486 9 Solos........................$8.99

SONATINA HUMORESQUE
Late Intermediate Level
00296772 3 Movements..............$6.99

SONGS WITHOUT WORDS
Intermediate Level
00296506 9 Solos........................$9.99

THREE PRELUDES
Early Advanced Level
00130747 3 Solos........................$8.99

THROUGHOUT THE YEAR
Late Elementary Level
00296723 12 Duets.....................$6.95

ADDITIONAL COLLECTIONS

AT THE LAKE
by Elvina Pearce
Elementary/Late Elementary Level
00131642 10 Solos and Duets.....$7.99

CHRISTMAS FOR TWO
by Dan Fox
Early Intermediate Level
00290069 13 Duets.....................$8.99

CHRISTMAS JAZZ
by Mike Springer
Intermediate Level
00296525 6 Solos........................$8.99

COUNTY RAGTIME FESTIVAL
by Fred Kern
Intermediate Level
00296882 7 Solos........................$7.99

LITTLE JAZZERS
by Jennifer Watts
Elementary/Late Elementary Level
00154573 9 Solos........................$8.99

PLAY THE BLUES!
by Luann Carman
Early Intermediate Level
00296357 10 Solos......................$9.99

ROLLER COASTERS & RIDES
by Jennifer & Mike Watts
Intermediate Level
00131144 8 Duets.......................$8.99

www.halleonard.com

Prices, contents, and availability subject
to change without notice.

0321
144